The Legacy Letters

The prompted journal for those who inspire us

Carrie Lloyd

Grace & Down
PUBLISHING

First published 2021 by Grace & Down Publishing, an imprint of
Malcolm Down Publishing Ltd.
www.malcolmdown.co.uk

24 23 22 21   7 6 5 4 3 2 1

British Library Cataloguing in Publication Data
A catalogue record for this book is available from the British Library.

ISBN 978-1-912863-95-2

Unless otherwise indicated, Scripture quotations taken from

Cover design by Alex Woodbury
Art direction by Sarah Grace

Printed in the UK

For Lilibet, Mrs Tiggywinkles,
Mamma-May, The Bestest Bestie,
'The Rev', Boofles…

Also known as…

My mother.

Chapters

Introduction

A Letter to the Writer

Childhood

Spirituality

Achievements

Adversity

Then and Now

Love

Memories and Stories

10 Favorites

"If I Could Do It Again"

Principles To Live By

Introduction

A few years ago I gave my mother a personalized leather-bound notebook for her birthday. This wasn't just a blank notebook, this was a book in which I wanted her to fill the pages about her life, her thoughts, her motivations, her principles, her favorite memories. I gave her themes, sections, questions and musings to ponder on.

They were the questions I wish I had asked my father before he died.

Since she received this book, the pages have been filled with her favorite recipes, sketches, photographs of the old air raid shelter she and her brother played in just after the war. It has that fruit cake recipe whereby the entire thing is devoured by the afternoon. I discovered that my father had been engaged before my mother, but despite her dashing looks, he didn't engage in conversation like he did with Mum that one time in the college canteen.

I learned more about my mother in the pages of this book than I had in 40 years of my life with her. It seems that whether it is our parents or someone that holds a significant influence and inspiration over us, we deem them to be invincible, we think we'll learn such information through osmosis, and forget to ask the questions. Perhaps we mean to dig deeper and seek to go back in history with those we love, but we leave it a little too late, when the memories have faded, when they don't remember the details anymore.

The digital age spoon feeds us information that makes us believe we are beyond teachable from our ancestors, that we can learn all there is to know from a TikTok video. It ignores the understanding that every person has their own unique story, their own set of principles that could be gifts for those who are watching close by. Our own roots and influences become far more compelling when we ask intimate questions of those who raised us, those who guided us. They are in our lives for a reason. They were there for us to learn from. And as I turn forty, I'm aware that if we are not careful, we could miss the very gift that was intended for us and us alone – their legacy.

Anyone who has experienced loss will now have faced the realism of mortality: the limited time that we each have on the earth. Legacy in this instance is the imparting not just of inheritance or financial property, but a bespoke wisdom, crafted and molded by life's hurdles. The necessary suffering that created their wisdom is unique to their story.

Why is it that we have so many questions after they died that we didn't ask before? In the loss of someone that has gone before us, is the birth of intrigue, of nostalgia – this was the reason alone for The Legacy Letters, so that we wouldn't miss the opportunity to learn not just the hobbies, or the favorite poems of those who go before us, but the learnings, the regrets, the deeper questions and lessons of life that shouldn't be kept to their own graves. Such findings, such lessons from love and loss, should live on through us.

My fear in writing this book and giving it to someone significant in our life was that it might come across as a subconscious sentiment of 'In case you snuff it soon, write out all the things we need to know so that I do an above-adequate job of your eulogy.' I was worried in giving my mother a blank notebook, or recording her voice on my Dictaphone, that she'd think she was some walking Morrie, expecting me to carry out some 'living funeral' just like the book *Tuesdays with Morrie* by Mitch Albom embraced.

Thankfully she understood the real meaning to my madness.

I didn't want to miss her. I don't mean that definition to mean 'long or pine for her after she left the earth.' I meant I didn't want to miss the substance of her. The entirety of her. What made her gentle, what made her sharp. Where did she find this acerbic humor that my cousins and I would write down when she came out with a corker of a line? What caused her to pick fights when she was naturally a peacemaker? The virtues I envied in her were clearly inspired examples of what I needed to learn. And if I didn't ask the questions, I was never going to know. Observing her wasn't enough. Going on trips with her wasn't enough. Assuming she did things from my own eye witness account was a terrible plan, because as these questions came out, so too did I learn how wrong my assumptions were. How rarely I had the real context for why she did what she did.

When I learned that my father had been engaged before he met my mother, and the reason why that first engagement didn't end well was because this beautiful 60s model had 'nothing between the ears.' Bit harsh, I thought, but dang I wished I had known. Perhaps I could have avoided similar choices I had made with dashing men in my twenties.

Equally as these stories created their own confessional declarations from my mother, friends were losing their fathers, at far too early an age. Both to cancer. Both wild in personality and character. Both successful and brilliant story tellers. Both hadn't written down much in the way of tales from post-war, or learnings from their childhood. Unless it had randomly risen in conversation over dinner, unless my friends had intentionally asked them to recite the lessons of their life, the stories were lost in the ether.

'I'm sad,' my friend said, 'that it not only took cancer for me to dig deeper into the character of my father, but that I left it too late into the illness, that the book I did give him to fill out is still empty, so now there is an entire history of ancestral stories from the war, from hardship, from young love, that my children will never know about their grandfather. That I'll never know of my father.'

Regardless of this hardwired approach of our parents and even grandparents' invincibility, a survival tactic perhaps in our earlier years, the questions did not only teach us something from them, but the most fascinating discovery was that in testing this approach with my mother, she had not asked herself these questions. She had not sat down to think beyond her every day.

The Legacy Letters became then not just a gift for our own guidance, but they discovered themselves. For the first time, especially for a generation older than us who were taught to keep busy, to not be too self-indulgent, to not get introspective, this was perhaps the only counselling session they were willing to have – because it came with the argument that it would help us. But truly, in this uncovering, in these stories, there was an acceptance, as well as a celebration, of the amount that they had learned, the power which had strengthened them, and that no amount of success or wealth substantiates legacy necessarily. Legacy was built on the fabric of life itself. What built the character of anyone who reached the mountain top was not the accomplishments but the hurdles, the adversity, the love found and lost, the tragedy as well as the wins. There is a gift in it all, for both their hearts to discover now, in the peace and silence of our encouragement to learn, and our own hearts towards knowing we left no stone unturned.

A Letter To The Writer
(The one who has been given this book)

Y ou must have done something right in your life to receive this book, for this is only given to those who have already inspired us, the ones who lead a life full of color and experience – to write your findings, your learnings, your wisdom.

As we tested this book, we noticed a few things that might be worth taking note of before you begin. In this day and age, we are fed so much information we are not given much time to ask questions, to seek out our own ideologies or quest for connection with others.

This book endeavors to ask you questions that you may not have been asked before, the answers to which may take some guts. Some digging deeper into the reflections of your life. This isn't necessarily meant to be an easy read book, for I too shall prepare the receiver, the one you gift this back to, with some resilience to withstand all that you may share and divulge.

The first thing to note is to ensure it is honest. Don't answer it with things you believe we might want to hear, answer it with a brutal honesty that will give us insight, insight for our own future. Additionally with this honesty, ensure that there is honor for all those mentioned. If there have been affairs or criminal activity, this book perhaps should not be the first place to divulge that. Reference such moments for a further conversation, and let not names be exposed within the pages. The pages are purely your own learnings of what you deciphered in the journey. Lessons you wish you had been told.

This is not so much a confessional as a reflection from previous confessionals – a space for you to reflect on your life with all the knowledge you have now. Take your time in answering, don't rush nor feel the need to write the first thing that comes to mind.

The younger generations have been more earnest for their former generation to be vulnerable. Please push pass any nerves that may filter too much, nerves that would leave us only having more questions. This is a humble venture, for both the writer and the reader. The questions were designed to dive deeper into the ocean of your life, for we have become tired of swimming around the surface.

The legacy in which you hold, will be treasured amid these pages. Let every answer be a gift to the reader, let every question be a gift for your own self-discovery.

Above all, let your heart and life speak, reach for the details that you may deem unnecessary, for they may very well be a key for us to carry further into our humble existence.

Carrie

Childhood

"I took you to your first musical when you were five. A moment I was anticipating greatly, as you loved to dance on the furniture and create your 'shows' in the living room. But when it came to the arts, you couldn't stand the dialogue, and so would take a mince pie out of the bag I gave you and throw it in the air, catching it up in the paper bag – in the middle of the audience, all whilst the actors talked. When the music and dancing numbers began, you were all eyes on the stage. Needless to say, I didn't take you again until you stopped eating mince pies."

– Carrie's mother

Childhood is not just the shaping of us, it also shows the early stages of what we were wired with. Whether those unique intricacies are nurtured or dismissed are another story, but what we learn in this chapter of you will be very telling for us. What built you, what crushed you, and what formed the great character we now know.

What was your childhood like?

What is your favorite memory from your childhood?

What was the most trouble you got into when you were a teenager?

Did you have a favorite pet? Why were they your favorite?

Who, in your childhood, taught you about love, and what did you learn?

What was the greatest hurdle of your childhood and how did you overcome it?

How many children did you want when you grew up?

Did you have a specific plan?

Were there any hurdles in having your own family? If so, what were they?

How did you find strength to persevere in raising a family,

when things were tough?

Have you copied or followed similar ways of loving people/your family the same way you were loved? Have you changed anything out of principle?

What advice would you give someone in raising children?

(This can still be answered from a place of observation if you didn't

have any children of your own)

What do you think about how children are being raised in the world today?

Spirituality

It was not until I sat in silence for 8 days, it was not until I let the world finally speak, that I discovered the necessity of the spirit, and all it could do when I said yes to it. But first, I had to let go of me. All of me.

People have lived and died by their faith. Some were raised with a very different form of understanding of God than what they died believing. We have seen people stand in great and noble tasks, not by their own free will but because of a surrender to their faith. In order to fully understand your actions, your motivations, we must ask your why, and it is here, amid the faith or the supernatural, that we shall discover an essence of who you are.

What is your understanding of God?

What does your spiritual life look like?

How do you integrate your faith into your life?

How do your beliefs shape you?

Did you have any phase in your life where your faith
or spirituality were different?

What is your favorite testimony from your faith?

What is your favorite teaching?

What is your favorite scripture? Do you have a favorite quote?

Do you believe in miracles? Have you witnessed any personally?

Did any particular event or story change your mind around your spirituality?

What is the moment you felt closest to God?

What is the greatest gift your spirituality has provided?

What would you say to those in your life who want to be more spiritual?

What has changed in your understanding of God over your life?
Has it remained the same throughout?

When was your spirituality or faith tested most?

Achievements

To overcome, might be the greatest achievement of all.

There are the awards, the shiny trophies, the medals, the accolades that adorn one's mantel piece. But there is also that personal sense of achievement: the crossword puzzle you accomplished without the aid of Mr. Google, that grouting you finally got finished, or dare I say it, that argument over the growing buddleia from your neighbor's garden which found resolution. Whatever they are, none should be measured against the other, all should be praised for one thing only: the perseverance you grasped for having achieved it at all.

Personally, what do you believe have been your greatest achievements?

Was there a moment where you truly experienced your greatest victory?

Were there any achievements you really wanted to accomplish
but life took a different turn? If so, what happened?

What dreams did you have when you were younger?
Which ones were fulfilled and which ones never came to being?

Academically and/or professionally, what have been
your greatest achievements?

In your personal relationships, what has been your greatest victory?

Was there an accolade you received that you felt you didn't deserve?

Was there an accolade you didn't receive that you felt
as though you should have?

What was your metaphorical Everest, and were you able to climb it?

Adversity

You might laugh in the face of adversity, but have you ever encountered the 405 on a Friday night in L.A? That'll sweep the giggles from your lungs.

Borderline Millennials, and the generations before, may remember the times when renting a newly released film from Blockbuster was an entire event. We would discuss at length before getting into our car to make our fateful journey, what film we'd like to watch and if it had sold out, because it's Saturday night, what would our second and third options be? We'd have to settle for the bargain bin films due to the high demand whilst also being reminded to rewind the VHS tape and ensure it wasn't returned late – if it was, you had a late fee. Many minor compromises we had to make in our day have been removed thanks to technology and the digital age. However, life itself still brings us adversity. This is where your wisdom comes in, and why we must be reminded of the greater challenges you might have faced, so that we never take advantage of the ease set before us.

What has been the greatest hurdle you have ever had to face?

What helped you get through this time?

Who helped you in your life when facing adversity?

Did anyone or anything hinder you from achieving what you truly desired?

Did you gain anything from these darker hours?

What should we do with adversity? How should we face it?

How is it best, in your opinion, to process pain?

Who is the bravest person you know and why?

Were you ever frightened of being rejected?

Or being so vulnerable with someone that they could break your heart?

What choices, or circumstances, built courage in you?

What helps you in a difficult time?

How do you help others when they are facing their darkest times?

Are there any practical things that help you
or a friend through a grieving period?

What lessons did you learn from grief?

When you were hurt, how did you forgive them?

What is the greatest thing you had to forgive?

Has there been an event that you were never able to forgive or let go of?

Then and Now

Even if your great grandfather's first automobile was a Penny Farthing, has anything really ever changed, at least with the very substance of people?

Fireside chats with our relatives often discuss the changes of time: the war, post war, the information age, the influencer age. When witnessing a person receive a telegram from the Queen for their 100th birthday, the happy learnings from then until now, may always make us happy that we live in the present. But sometimes, when we look back to then, the purity of relationships, the present-nature of conversation, the hard graft that had to be garnered by our grandparents, may very well be inspirations for us now – in a search to regain that which was lost.

What has been the biggest change in your lifetime?

What do you miss the most from your former times?

What don't you miss at all?

How has technology changed over the years for you?

How has this affected your life and those around you?

How has dating differed from your generation to my
generation over your lifetime?

What has changed in the concept of family since you grew up in one?

Tell me a day in the life of your childhood.
What were your daily tasks like compared to now?
What took the most time?

What is the most significant change in you – then to now? What has changed?
What has stayed the same?

What did you hope would change but hasn't, or worse,
has deteriorated in this generation?

What do you think we should bring back (be it technology, a type of music, or a governmental bill) that would revolutionize this generation?

Love

⁓

Love? Oh darling, that's a quandary that only those who have overcome it, surrendered to it, and been completely devoured by it, could comment. I've only been devoured by its' hunt.

I am yet to surrender to it with an ally.

There are many components to break down the understanding of love. In addition to C.S Lewis' 'Four Loves,' it is expressed in many forms and is required in many settings, not just in the stance of romance or marriage, but through our childhood, and in forgiving others. This chapter looks at the mystery of love. But please, no holding back. Your stories of redemption will bring us hope on our darker days.

What does love mean to you?

Who taught you about love, and what were the principles
you learned from them?

What does love look like in the small every day moments?

What's your personal greatest love story?

What are your thoughts on romance? Is it rational? Can you be wise and in love at the same time?

Did you have any rules or restraints when it came to dating and courtship?

Was there a relationship you regret ending? If so, why?

Is there a difference between infatuation and love?
If so, what are the differences?

Do you believe in the concept of 'The One?'

If married, how did you know your spouse was the one to marry?
If you remained single, what were the blessings of going solo?

Describe the day of your wedding: morning, the ceremony and night.

Was your love passionate and instant, or did it grow over time?

What are the fundamental principles you live by to keep
your marriage successful/happy?

How important is it to marry at all?

Being vulnerable and whole-hearted with someone
can be scary, were you afraid of being hurt?

How did you navigate ensuring each other still fulfilled their dreams?
Does someone always have to 'concede' to the other's dreams?

What has been your experience in the realm of heartbreak? Would you do anything differently after learning about heartbreak?

How do we find courage to walk away or let go of people
when love is calling you in a different direction?

How have you kept loving people even if they are intentionally or unintentionally choosing to hurt?

When is it best to end a relationship?

What do boundaries look like to you when it comes to love?
Do you have a limit of how much you let someone into your world?

Memories and Stories

"When we ran the 171 club in 1968, we had a tuck shop that sold Wagon Wheels and Vimto soda. But we had to get the cats in to clear out the rats every night before we opened. Health and Safety wouldn't have had as much of a sense of humor as we did, of course."
– Carrie's mother

The anecdotes, the hilarious stories you tell over again at dinner, the memories that you wish to cherish along with the inspired stories that changed your life – these are the making of passions themselves, ones to live by, ones we hoped to be inspired by, or equally amused.

What was your first day at high school like?

Do you have a favorite love story of another – can be both fictional or one you witnessed?

What is your favorite story you have retold a hundred times over dinner?

What's your favorite supernatural story?

When were you most scared?

Was there a day in history that you were a part of, or a close witness to? If so, what did that look like?

When did you feel the most safe?

Was there one single day that entirely changed your life?

What day was your happiest?

When where you most embarrassed?

What is the strangest thing that has ever happened to you?

Have you ever been or been close to being arrested?

Who is the one who got away?

Have you ever met one of your heroes?

Have you ever nearly lost your life?

Have you ever saved a life?

If you could repeat one day, what would it be?

10 Favorites

Carrie's Mother's Best Cake Recipe:

Ingredients: 200g sultanas or other mixed fruit, 250ml milk, 200g sugar, 125g soft margarine/butter, 250g self-raising flour, 1 egg, 1 teaspoon of cinnamon or mixed spice (optional)

Instructions: Put the dried fruit, milk, butter and sugar into a saucepan and bring to the boil, stirring all the time. Once boiled, turn off the heat and allow to cool for 10 minutes. Fold in the flour and mix well, then add the egg and mix again. Pour into a 2lb loaf tin (I use a paper liner) and put in an oven preheated to 160°C for an hour.

This is easy to make and more or less foolproof. It can be eaten hot with custard, as a snack, or as part of an afternoon tea. I once forgot to put the egg in, and it did not seem to make any difference! I also reduce the sugar as much as possible. (But you can overdo it!) You can add fresh blueberries, raspberries and strawberries right at the end, or ginger, rum – whatever you like. It is a very user-friendly cake!

Well, we couldn't just leave it to one favorite, could we? You may enjoy adding some extras here – in the way that my mother added recipes, sketches, photos etc. Please enjoy her cake recipe, and feel free to add your own.

Top 10 Favorite Films

Top 10 Favorite Books

Top 10 Favorite Songs

Top 10 Favorite TV Shows

Top 10 Favorite Theatre Shows

Top 10 Favorite Quotes

Top 10 Favorite Artists

Top 10 Favorite Comedians

Top 10 Favorite Jokes

Top 10 Favorite Recipes
(feel free to add pages or cards to this page)

Top 10 Favorite Towns or Places

Top 10 Most Inspirational People

"If I Could Do It Again"

───ᨍ───

I would ask more questions, tell more jokes, laugh more in the face of adversity, see problems as opportunities, and take more time to tell people I loved them. Thank God there is time, given that I'm only 41.

Would you have done anything differently in the name of love?

Would you have done anything differently with regards to family?

Would you have done anything differently in your career(s)?

Would you have done anything differently for your health?

If you could travel back in time and give your 20-year-old self some advice, what would it be?

What is your greatest regret?

What was your biggest gamble? Did it pay off?

Is there anything you never got the chance to say?
What was it, and to whom would you say it?

What should you have worried about more and what
should you have worried about less?

If there was one thing you could change about yourself, what would it be?

Principles to Live By
(by that I mean, "Principles by which to live")

———

Principles? I finally found them. Somewhere between my humility and supper nights around the dining table. Such principles saved me causing many hurts to others. I hope.

What was the best principle of life that you were taught?

What would be your advice to me on love and romance?

What do you believe to be the greatest misconceptions on love?

What should we do if we make a mistake?

What daily rituals have helped you in your life?

Do you have a favorite proverb or go-to lifeline quote?

What would you want to hear if you were standing at the pearly gates
(or the other spot)?

How much of ourselves should we sacrifice?
Is there such a thing as too much?

What advice do you believe I need to hear most?

To Conclude

A s the stories unfold, as the pages turn over, as the revelations of past and present come to fruition and create new questions, may they form stronger bonds and more questions to continue this wonder from one generation to another.

May this be a starting point, not a place to close the exploration of each other.

The beauty of a legacy is that it is forever changing, forever traditional but adaptable to the person carrying on the legacy. It is moldable to work with the changing of the age, but loyal to the core principles of those who gained the wisdom in the first place. We can be reminded in these pages that we are metaphorically holding the hand of those who trod the path before us, whilst we are led to discover our own.

I hope that you discovered, after both writing and reading the answers, the depth and insight to the person you were already intrigued by. That conversations over a cuppa may leave you feeling not just inspired, but charged to relish the power of a person who seeks to give back to the next generation and not just let their findings stay with themselves.

We are in an era where we seek comfort over sacrifice, selfish desires over the joy for another, and it is here, where the writer hopefully stretched beyond their comfort zone to give the reader some powerful lessons, as well as fabulous supper time stories, and the reader accepted gracefully the truth that fell upon the pages. It is my hope that, as the reader receives these learnings, they too find opportunities to thank, empower and embrace the very brilliance of the writer's unique stories.

That is the beauty and power of the legacy: it is individual, colorful and original to everyone who shares their life with someone who dug a little deeper than the small talkers at the bar.

The Legacy Letters not only wished to create a record of original thought from the writer, but a bond between both the reader and the writer, greater than it was before you opened this book.

With love, light and their legacy,

Carrie

About the Author

Carrie Lloyd is the host of 'The Carrie On…podcast', journalist, Patreon writer and life guide, specialising in authenticity, character and therefore, love. She is the author of three books: *The Noble Renaissance* (Harper Collins), *The Virgin Monologues*, and *Prude*. Carrie resides between her homes in California, where she is a foster mother, and Lincolnshire, England.

The Virgin Monologues

How can you thrive in a predominately secular culture and keep your faith in a world that doesn't reflect your values?

The Virgin Monologues teaches how to do healthy relationships, what to fight for and what to give up on. It gives healthy principles to understand before looking for a soul mate. Carrie shows how you, as a single Christian woman, can maintain your relationships while staying true to yourself.

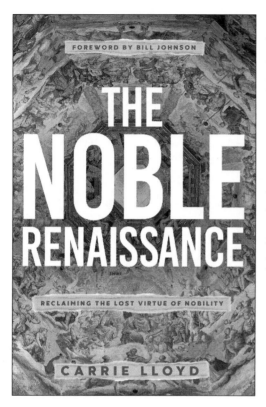

Do you ever wonder who you are, why you are here, and what really makes life worth living? Or perhaps something is holding you back from believing you could be a person who can make a real difference in the world. In The Noble Renaissance, author and life coach Carrie Lloyd challenges you to be done with pretending, be done with striving, be done with religion—and develop a noble character that truly reflects the person of Christ.

Made in United States
Orlando, FL
09 December 2022